AuthorPreneur Elite

By

Raza Imam

www.AuthorPreneurElite.com

MATERIAL CONNECTION DISCLOSURE: You should assume that the author of this book has an affiliate relationship and/or another material connection to the providers of goods and services mentioned in this message and may be compensated when you purchase from a provider. You should always perform due diligence before buying anything online or offline.

TABLE OF CONTENTS

NEED ADVICE? REACH OUT TO ME 1

FREE VIDEO CASE STUDY 3

SHORT AND SWEET *(BECAUSE WE'RE ALL BUSY)* . 5

MY STORY 9

SECTION 1 12

THE *PROBLEM* AND THE *POTENTIAL*

Is This Book Even For YOU?

The "Coaching/Consulting Curse" (the BIGGEST problem with being an "expert")

This Is RIDICULOUS (there IS a better way…)

Grow Your Business As An Elite "AuthorPreneur"

My Emotional Roller Coaster Ride As a Writer (and what you can learn from it)

Still Not Convinced? (you will be)

SECTION 2 62

THE "RWPPPP" PROCESS

Research (the most underestimated step)

Writing (how to write an awesome non-fiction book in 24 hours)

Positioning (how to blow your competition out of the water)

Profit on Backend (this is where the real money is made)

Publish (bring your book to life)

Promotion (launch like a Hollywood blockbuster)

SECTION 3 132

THE 7 P'S OF LONG-TERM PROMOTION

The Launch "Hangover"

Paid Ads to Promote Your Book (this is a must for ongoing sales)

Podcasts Interviews and Partners to Promote Your Book (this is hot, hot, hot)

Press and Media (use your book to become a media celebrity)

Post on Social Media (the secret of repurposing your book)

Professional Associations and Podiums (this is how the big dogs do it)

Personal Outreach (this is how you really differentiate yourself)

CONCLUSION *(TIME IS OF THE ESSENCE)* 167

RECOMMENDED RESOURCES 170

NEED ADVICE? REACH OUT TO ME 172

HOW I CAN HELP 173

BEFORE YOU LEAVE A REVIEW…........................... 175

Need Advice? Reach Out To Me

If you need personal advice on your project, feel free to contact me in one of the following ways:

Email: Feel free to email me directly at raza.imam@authorpreneurelite.com

Facebook Group: Feel free to join my free Facebook Group http://authorpreneurelite.com/fbgroup to ask questions and interact with the community. I share videos and helpful tips here.

LinkedIn: Feel free to connect with me and ask me questions on LinkedIn at www.LinkedIn.com/in/razasimam I also share videos and tips here.

Book a Call: If you want to schedule time for me to give you personal advice (*for free*), feel free to book time on my calendar here to learn more about how I can help:

www.authorpreneurelite.com/discovery-call

I read every email and am really excited to help you.

Free Video Case Study

I recorded an in-depth, 30-minute video explaining the details of how you can use my "*AuthorPreneur Elite*" system to earn passive income by turning your expertise into highly-profitable books, online courses, coaching, consulting, and speaking.

Here are the 3 secrets you'll discover:

- **Secret #1: The "Spy Method" to See What's Already Selling Well**: You'll be _shocked_ when you see how powerful this is (*Amazon does all of the work for you*)

- **Secret #2: The "Give 'Em What They Want" Method**: This secret _alone_ is worth watching this video you'll learn how to tap into your reader's _deepest_ desires so they can't help but buy from you

- **Secret #3: The "Hollywood Launch" to Trigger Massive Sales**: My _secret strategy_ to launch books to #1 bestseller status; earn passive income from royalties and sell *highly-profitable* courses, consulting, and speaking

I'll even send you an 11-page pdf cheat sheet that summarizes the entire process afterward.

Just download the free cheat sheet here and videos here:

www.AuthorPreneurElite.com

I've given you all the steps you need to get started, but if you ever need help, feel free to email me at raza.imam@authorpreneurelite.com so my team and I can help.

Short and Sweet *(Because We're All Busy)*

"Give me a one-page bullet-list of exactly what I should do. That's worth more to me than a stack of books that I have to dig through to get to the good stuff. I may give you 50 bucks for the books. But I'll pay you $5,000 for the one page."

-Alwyn Cosgrove, fitness coach, trainer, entrepreneur

You're busy.

I'm busy.

We're all busy.

It's an epidemic of the modern age.

That's why I kept this book short and sweet.

It's practical, it's tactical, and it's actionable.

Why?

Because I want to give you the meat and potatoes so that you can get started and take things to the next level - as soon as possible.

Because if you're like me, time is your most valuable asset.

Honestly, who actually has time to read 200-300 page books? With 3 young kids that need my attention, I sure don't!

It's also why CEOs have executive summaries prepared for them. Rather than spending hours and hours pouring over detailed reports, they need the most valuable information, distilled into actionable insights, so that they can make critical decisions and take action.

That's what I want for you.

You'll notice that there's a lot that I ***don't*** talk about in this book; that's for a reason.

My goal is to give you the quickest, easiest, simplest way to find leads and make sales using the power of a book.

That's why I called it "*AuthorPreneur Elite*".

Attention: I Write Short Paragraphs

Please note, I write in short, punchy paragraphs that are usually one or two sentences long.

Why?

Because I write for the internet.

You see, some of the biggest, most popular websites in the world write in short, one to three sentence paragraphs, from [TechCrunch](), to [Mashable](), to [CopyBlogger](), [to Smashing Magazine](), to [The Huffington Post](), to [TheBlaze]().

They do this because it makes it much easier to read; apparently the extra white space is easier on the eyes.

I do it because I find that it's easier for me to crank out ideas.

When I write, I write from the heart and writing short paragraphs like this is a part of that.

I hope you enjoy reading this book as much as I enjoyed writing it.

If you do like it, please send me feedback at raza.imam@authorpreneurelite.com

I'd love to hear from you.

MY STORY

Before we go on, I'd like to tell you a little bit about myself and how I can help you.

At the time of this writing, I'm 38 years old with a wife and 3 children (12, 8, and 3).

My mother had her own business for most of my life, so I've been entrepreneurial since an early age. In college, a friend and I started a software development company for large manufacturing companies. We eventually started doing software work for small startup companies and brought the business to about $30k/month in revenue.

But since we were both young and inexperienced, the business eventually folded and my partner and I parted ways.

But one thing I did learn from having my own company at such a young age was how to market myself online. From blogging, to search engine optimization, to email marketing, to copywriting, to sales funnels, to lead generation, to market research.

I also learned that most consultants struggle with generating consistent leads, so I definitely wasn't alone.

After that, I spent over a decade in healthcare IT, working for the largest hospital system in Illinois. I trained doctors and managed multi-million dollar software implementations. I supported thousands and thousands of medical assistants, nurses, and physicians.

Since I had an entrepreneurial spirit, I continued to start and test different business ideas - all while holding down a full-time job.

Eventually, I stumbled upon the power of self-publishing on Amazon. I discovered how to launch a book to bestseller status, and then use that to offer my readers high-value products and services like consulting, coaching, speaking, and online courses.

It all comes down to positioning yourself as an expert, building your authority, and demonstrating your expertise with a well-written book.

Over time, I've been able to help highly-skilled experts such as psychologists, corporate consultants, CEO's, and executive coaches position themselves as experts and attract high-value clients and lucrative speaking and profitable partnerships.

I will use my decades of marketing experience, as well as my 10+ years as a corporate healthcare consultant to refine your positioning and master your messaging so that you dominate your industry, position yourself as an expert, highlight your expertise, and build your authority - all with the power of a book.

SECTION 1

The *Problem* and the *Potential*

Is This Book Even For <u>YOU?</u>

Before you go any further, I want to tell you that I wrote this book for **<u>you</u>**.

IF....

If you're a highly-skilled expert that provides a transformative business result, like social media marketing, or coaching female executives to earn more money, or passing a professional certification (like project management, accounting, etc.), or starting a successful franchise, or helping companies attract and retain high-performing employees, or successfully raising capital, or guiding entrepreneurs through selling their companies, etc. then this book is for **<u>you</u>**.

If you've experienced a personal transformation like turning around a struggling relationship, or getting in shape, or helping people become more confident, or successfully coping with depression, or helping a friend through substance abuse, or becoming a more engaged parent, or time management and productivity techniques, or how to buy your first house, etc. then this book is for **you**.

The key is that you have the knowledge, expertise, and authority to help achieve a transformative personal or business result. You don't necessarily have to be a certified "expert", but you do have to have a story that you can share with others and a plan for how to help others.

You've got to be able to identify with your target market, deeply understand their problems, pains, and challenges, and have a high level of empathy. You also have to be able to show them how you can help with story, imagery, and emotion.

Over the past 2 years, I've personally worked with:

- Content marketing experts
- Career coaches
- Nationally-recognized marriage counselors
- Local and national media consultants
- Award-winning mortgage brokers

- Fortune 500 executive coaches
- Healthcare and hospital consultants
- CEO's of marketing companies
- Ivy-league psychologists
- Sports performance and mindset coaches
- Technology executives
- CEO's of software companies
- Doctors
- College consultants
- Directors of Fortune 500 companies
- Customer experience experts
- IT Security consultants to billion-dollar companies
- Instagram marketing experts
- Ecommerce marketing experts

Each of these people had an incredibly high-value skill that transformed people's lives - personal and business - in very powerful ways. And they wanted to know how to turn their expertise into a book that attracted more leads, clients, and sales.

They wanted to know how to turn their expertise into a product so that they could sell more of their high-value consulting, speaking, and online courses - ***without*** overwhelm, stress, or frustration.

Maybe you're in the same boat?

You have ***very*** specialized expertise and *you know* you should be monetizing it through a book, online course, or digital product, but you're not sure how to get started...

Maybe you've been wondering...

"How do I get a steady, reliable stream of high-value clients that will pay me a premium price for the service I provide?"

"How do I build an audience of highly-motivated prospects that are eager for what I have to offer?"

"How do I become the trusted go-to expert in my industry so I'm recognized for my authority, credibility, and expertise?"

"How can I consult with larger, more affluent clients that seek me out for my expertise - without cold calling and constantly networking?"

If you're wondering about any of this, then keep reading because **_this book is for you_**.

The "Coaching/Consulting Curse" *(the BIGGEST problem with being an "expert")*

Almost every week I speak to coaches, consultants, and speakers that have an amazing skill, experience, or knowledge that provide powerful transformations for their clients; but **_no_** idea how to market it.

The other day I spoke to a female executive coach. She was a University of Michigan engineering grad, got her MBA from Columbia, and worked at PepsiCo and CocaCola.

VERY impressive.

But she's not getting as many clients as she'd like.

Big problem.

Before that, I spoke to a healthcare consultant that helps hospitals with organizational change and development. He has a Ph.D. and is highly accomplished in his field.

But he's tired of chasing his clients and collecting payments.

<u>Big</u> problem.

I have a friend that is a corporate security consultant. He advises billion-dollar companies on their cybersecurity and risk assessment plans to protect them from hackers and fraudsters.

He's amazing at what he does but hates having to constantly sell to get new clients.

<u>Big</u> problem.

I spoke to another client that was a physician. He wanted to help people live happier, healthier lives and tour the country showing them how to sleep better, combat stress and anxiety, and prolong their lives.

But he didn't know how to promote his message.

<u>Big</u> problem.

I could give even more examples, but I hope you see the problem that I'm referring to.

You see, each of these individuals is a ***highly*** skilled expert.

They've gone to the top schools in the country. They've worked for the most prestigious companies. They are doing amazing work. They deliver profitable, life-changing results.

But despite them being highly educated, experienced, and accomplished, they were never taught how to promote themselves.

It's like opening an award-winning restaurant in the middle of the jungle; it doesn't matter how good it is if there are no people there.

To me, that's a tragic situation because they have the potential to affect so many lives with their expertise, authority, and knowledge.

Instead, they're struggling to make their message heard.

They want to boost their authority.

They want to demonstrate their credibility.

They want to break out of a rut.

They want to convey their expertise.

They want to differentiate themselves.

They want high-value clients coming to them.

They yearn to be acknowledged as the experts that they are in their industry.

These are big problems, but the beauty is that there is a simple, elegant, preeminent solution that solves all of these problems (quite handily I might add)

It's to write a book!

And I'm not talking about a 300-page brick that no one has time to read either.

I'm talking about a hard-hitting, 75-150 page book that defines a very specific problem and shows how to solve it with story, imagery, and emotion.

The good news is that these experts already had speeches, white papers, presentations, articles, blog posts, and notes that they had already written over the years that they are easily able to compile into a rough draft for a short, 75-150 page book.

All they needed was to know how ***simple*** it really is.

Consider this; the world's most recognized experts from every field you can possibly imagine, from astronomy, to acting, to marketing, to psychology, to sales, to relationships, to media and culture, to politics, to self-help, to parenting, to medicine, to programming, to entrepreneurship, all have cemented their authority by writing a book.

So why not you?

The entire point of this book is to show you how to take your expertise, envelop it in story, emotion, and imagery, and use that to connect with your ideal audience in as little time as possible.

So, are you a highly-skilled expert with a story to tell?

Are you relying on networking, referrals, and word of mouth to grow your coaching, consulting, or speaking business? Are you tired of trading time for dollars?

Have you ever wished you could monetize your expertise and turn it into a product like a book or online course that sells day in and day out, leading to steady, consistent income?

Or maybe you're a leadership consultant, or an executive coach, or a social media strategist, or a fitness expert.

Do you have life experiences, a personal transformation, or specialized expertise that can deliver results for people?

If so, then this book will help you go from being an expert to a ***recognized*** expert - FAST.

This Is RIDICULOUS
(there IS a better way…)

Quick story: (*this is absolutely ridiculous…*)

A few weeks ago, I saw an interview with a 21-year-old author from Singapore that makes $40k per month.

Of course, those are realistic numbers if you know what you're doing, but what shocked me was ***how*** he was doing it. Rather than writing a few books that position him as an authority, he writes little nonfiction books on a variety of topics and sells them on Amazon, IngramSpark, and Draft2Digital.

To the tune of $500,000 per year! (*well, $480k to be exact*)

But here's the kicker…

He started when he was 16 and over the past 5 years, he has published over 600 books! (*these are little books that he paid someone else to write*)

His mother was a business owner and fostered his entrepreneurial spirit. Once he learned how to do this, he started his mini-publishing business. Again, he didn't write the books, he just paid ghostwriters, slapped a pen name on them, and published them.

(*I'm teaching my 12 and 8 years old sons to start writing now too!*)

That means each book only makes $67 per month, or $2.00 per day (*a paltry sum if you ask me*)

But I know authors with similar business models. One guy has 100 books and makes about $15,000 per month.

He orders 3-5 books to be written at a time and publishes them every month. Within a few years, he's pumped out 100+ books (*30 of which make a bulk of his money*)

I was equally awed and inspired by his work ethic, drive, and ingenuity.

It kind of blew my mind, but I *know* it's possible because I see authors following a similar model.

They write about all kinds of obscure topics, hoping that people stumble upon them online and buy them. And since the books are so inexpensive, there's very little friction to buy.

In the early 2000s, online marketers employed a similar strategy called "Bum Marketing" or "Article Marketing". The premise was to publish a bunch of short, 500-word articles online about a variety of topics from gardening, to fitness, to getting your ex-lover back. It was called "bum marketing" because the idea was that even a bum can walk into a library, use a public computer, and write short little articles online with links to products that they can earn a commission on.

It goes to show that if you put your head down and WORK, you'll get amazing results.

While I respect the hustle, there ***is*** a BETTER way.

In a lot of ways, that's exactly what big publishing companies do. They pay authors to write books and then use their vast distribution network to publish the books online and get them prime positioning in bookstores and libraries.

Since you're already a highly-skilled expert, I want you to write a really good book that addresses the emotional needs of your target audience, launch it like a Hollywood blockbuster, use your "bestseller" status to get on the media and industry blogs and podcasts, and then sell high-end products and services (coaching, consulting, speaking, software, etc.) to your customers.

The potential is huge, and you can create something of real value if you do it right.

Maybe you've already written a book, but if you haven't yet, or if your book isn't generating the results you want, just know that the potential is HUGE.

Grow Your Business As An Elite "AuthorPreneur"

This book will show you how to turn your expertise into a non-fiction book that you can use to build your authority and scale your influence. But before we do that, it's instructive to see how fiction authors write and market their books - because many of them do it remarkably well. We'll then apply those lessons to your non-fiction book.

I know of independent, self-published *fiction* authors that make between $10,000 and $100,000 per month.

I know it sounds far-fetched and hard to believe... but it's 100% true.

These authors write books that people **_crave_**.

I'm talking about contemporary romance.

And science fiction space operas.

And investigative thrillers.

And most profitably of all, dirty, raunchy, erotica.

Their results are **_stunning_**.

They pump out books month after month and their readers **eat them up**.

There's an almost incessant desire for these topics, and readers respond by opening up their wallets and buying these books _by the truckload._

In fact, I was listening to a podcast where an author was talking about how he was making $60,000 per month by selling his self-published post-apocalyptic sci-fi novels on Amazon. It was so lucrative, that he turned down a 7-figure publishing deal, and decided to sail around the world.

The beauty is that a majority of these ebooks are sold and delivered electronically onto the reader's Kindle device.

He doesn't have to publish and print these books and rely on a publishing company to get them into bookstores.

He was able to rely on Amazon's vast infrastructure and audience to publish and distribute ebooks that his readers were addicted to.

Now I'm **_not_** saying that you should become a fiction author. I know **_nothing_** about it and don't have the creative genius to plot out a gripping story, with rich characters, an engaging story arc, and shocking climax.

But what I **_do_** know how to do is borrow the same engaging, compelling, evocative techniques that fiction authors use to write and promote hard-hitting nonfiction books.

And that's what I want to show you how to do in this book.

With that said, let's do something fun...

Just imagine for a moment that you were able to turn your expertise into a short, 75-150 page book and used it to build authority, credibility, and intimacy with your audience.

Then imagine using that authority to sell online courses, coaching, corporate consulting, and paid speaking.

They key is to write the book with empathy, where you share your story and identify with the _exact_ _same_ problems that your readers struggle with. If you can tap into your story and share your story, with imagery and emotion, you'll build a deep connection with your reader.

All of a sudden, your dry, technical non-fiction book starts to read like a gripping fiction novel with you as the protagonist and your story as the delivery mechanism to solve their problems.

The deeper you share your struggles, challenges, discoveries, breakthroughs, "aha" moments, your eventual success, the more emotional resonance you'll build with your readers.

You'll build trust if you can identify common pitfalls, obstacles, roadblocks, and challenges.

By sharing stories, they will not only have learned the dry, technical "how-to" information, they will have walked with you on your journey; from your struggles to your eventual triumphs.

Some of my favorite non-fiction books described the process in such vivid detail, with such graphic imagery, and such compelling realism, that they felt like I'm watching their story unfold in front of me like a play - which is motivating and inspires me to take action.

My favorite books made me feel as if I were traveling with them on their journey. They built such emotional intimacy that I saw myself in their story. They painted a picture of how I could transform my life through the imagery and emotion they conveyed... all of which caused me to take action.

It doesn't really matter what your expertise is, as long as you envelop it in _story_, use _imagery_, convey _emotion,_ and reveal how to deal with challenges; because that's what people _crave_.

It almost doesn't matter what you write about, as long as you convey it with story, imagery, and emotion.

From trying the keto diet; a good friend of mine is an ER doctor that gained a lot of weight because of the stress, but now swears by the keto diet (*and lost 80 pounds this way*)

To being a female entrepreneur; I recently spoke to a woman that was the first to go to college in her family, started a software company, and is successfully selling it (*and is now launching a female entrepreneurship coaching business*)

To putting yourself through college debt-free; I have a friend that was able to go to college in her 30's, while working a full-time job, for under $10,000 (*and she's at Harvard!*)

To selling a profitable software company; I have a friend that went from being divorced and broke to successfully selling an e-learning software company (*and incidentally started a new one*)

To successfully learning how to use social media for business (*a business coach of mine used LinkedIn to earn $150k in 90 days, and then showed others how to do the same*)

To learning how to be more focused and productive (*I know a guy that earns a 6-figure income writing about productivity*)

To helping corporate executives get promoted and land their dream job (*I know a woman that does this exact same thing*)

To training athletes to overcome negative self-talk, anxiety, and fear (*I know a coach that used his decades of experience as a coach to help young athletes*)

To leading and motivating a successful sales team (*I know a former corporate manager whose sales team consistently won sales awards by authentically, and compassionately leading them*)

Do you see what I did there?

Rather than just telling you that I know people who are fitness experts, or corporate consultants, or entrepreneurs, I included a key element of their story. I personalized and humanized them. I shared something unique, interesting, or compelling about them.

I know the claim of launching a book based on your expertise is hard to believe…

But I want you to suspend your disbelief for a moment.

Because a book is the _**#1**_ way to establish your credibility, authority, and expertise (next to being featured on Oprah... even then, a book will dramatically increase your chances!)

And I see people doing it every single day. I personally know:

- A young investor that quit his job and wrote a book and launched a coaching business that earned $100,000 in 30 days (*all of his leads came from his book*)

- A college student that turned his expertise into a book and earned passive income (*he earned $500-$800 per month in passive income*)

- A college professor and psychologist that turned his book into a consulting business (*he's used his book to speak at Google and on The Morning Show with Joe Scarborough*)

- A former physician that chose to become a conductor of a 200-member orchestra that now earns a six-figure income from her books and courses (*she performed in front of the Pope and at Carnegie Hall*)

- A former attorney that created a very lucrative publishing business writing about social skills and social interactions (*he now travels the world and releases a book every month*)
- And the list goes on...

The reason I went through these examples is that I want you to think like an entrepreneur, rather, an elite "authorpreneur".

I want you to think about how you can create value for others. I want you to look at yourself, your experience, your story, and your expertise as the product that others crave.

I want you to use a book to position yourself as the credible, authoritative, experienced expert that you are. And I want you to use that authority and credibility to sell high-value products and services that transform your readers' lives.

It's perfectly legitimate to wonder if writing a book is worth the effort.

The answer is a **resounding yes**, provided that you know what you are doing.

Later in this book, I'm going to share real-life examples of people earning an amazing living by simply sharing their expertise with the world.

All through a humble self-published book.

"So how do they earn their money?"

Great question.

Well, it comes from a lot of different sources:

- **Online Courses**: This is my favorite way to make money from a book. People have literally made millions of dollars selling online courses on topics as diverse as computer programming, debt reduction, putting babies to sleep, confidence, career change, public speaking, accounting, and online advertising.It is _extremely_ passive and _extremely_ profitable.

- **Coaching**: If you're a coach, you already know that high-ticket coaching is a very profitable business to be in. I offered one on one coaching before I created my first online course. When you consider how many people are willing to pay for an expert to coach them, it becomes easy to see why this is a fantastic way to make money.

- **Corporate Consulting**: If you blog about law, finance, accounting, marketing, or technology, your blog could provide a steady stream of high-paying corporate clients. Bloggers like Neil Patel, Chris Brogan, and others have earned millions of dollars by serving big corporations. Most of them have books that cemented their reputation.

- **Speaking Engagements**: Similar to corporate consulting, many authors make big money by speaking to corporations, industry associations, and at conferences. Imagine being paid $10,000 for a 45 minute speech to a group of corporate executives (it happens... a lot!)

- **Sell Products and Raise Funds**: Just look at what Tim Ferriss did with his dynamite book "*The 4-Hour Work Week*", or how Robert Kawasaki became a household name after writing "*Rich Dad, Poor Dad*", or how Eric Reis become a startup phenomenon after writing

"*The Lean Startup*", or how David Allan become the world's most popular productivity guru after writing "*Getting Things Done*". Just imagine the access to customers and investors they gained after publishing their books.

Each of these services could account for thousands (*often times <u>tens of thousands</u>*) of dollars to your bottom line **per month**.

When you think of it like that, you can start to see the potential.

Some people sell online courses that sell for $500-$1000. Some people offer corporate training for $10,000 to $15,000 per engagement. Some people speak and charge $10,000 to $25,000 per speech. Some people offer group coaching and charge $3,000 to $5,000 per client.

So rather than being an author, I want you to be an elite authorpreneur that builds a backend business with a mix of the offerings I mentioned above.

Imagine you write a book about female entrepreneurship and sell an online course about how career women can transition to entrepreneurship.

Or a niche course on Instagram marketing for ecommerce stores.

Or a course on public speaking for women.

Or imagine you write a book about sales performance and offer to train corporate sales teams.

Or what if you're an expert on putting babies to sleep and offer coaching to help new parents that are struggling as parents. (*My wife has personally bought a coaching package from a baby sleep coach.*)

What if you write a book about why software development projects fail and people contact you to help them with their failed projects?

So rather than asking "*Is it even possible to make money from a book?*" I want you to ask: "*What skills, talents, products, or services can I offer to people that solves a real problem that I can charge a premium price for?*"

Now you're thinking like an elite authorpreneur!

Key Points:

So, to end this chapter, let's quickly review a few things:

- Books _clearly_ will help you make a significant income

- But you **<u>have</u>** to write about something that people are interested in and are willing to pay money for

- You have to be credible, authentic, and honest

- You need to have a monetization strategy

All of the above strategies require you to have an audience (*it doesn't need to be huge*) to actually build your business.

So, don't start fantasizing about your fortune just yet, you need to read the rest of this book to find out how to write a book that attracts your ideal readers and inspires them to contact you.

My Emotional Roller Coaster Ride As a Writer *(and what you can <u>learn</u> from it)*

I've been entrepreneurial ever since I was 19. I had friends that went the med school and law school route who are now very successful doctors, lawyers, and dentists.

But I craved freedom and the ability to work on my own terms, so I chose to start a software development business with a friend.

It was HARD work, namely because I had no experience, credibility, or authority. I had to <u>*struggle*</u> to find clients. I'm talking about cold-calling and emailing companies desperately hoping that they'd respond to me.

It was draining and discouraging at times.

But then I got an idea; rather than trying to proverbially "knock on doors" until I got a response, I decided to start a blog dedicated to offshore outsourcing and all the things that go wrong with software development done overseas.

I called it SoftwareSweatshop.com (I shut the site down years ago) because I wanted it to be punchy, catchy, attention-grabbing, and unique.

Check.

Shortly after, interesting things started to happen; clients started finding me online via my blog (and hiring us to do work for them). I used my blog to get mentioned in Inc. Magazine and CIO.com.

I created little buttons that I would pin on my shirt and wear to networking events. *<u>It was a conversation starter for sure</u>*.

When I spoke to people I would tell them that I wrote about offshore software development and had an offshore development company. As a result, they would automatically ask me to help them with their projects.

SOFTWARE SWEATSHOP

www.software-sweatshop.com

(I created a button with this image and wore it at events, and it worked like a charm!)

It was amazing how well it worked to generate new clients.

Since I was in my early 20's and didn't have much actual experience, my business eventually fizzled out.

But it proved the importance of positioning myself to generate clients. I was able to differentiate myself by identifying problems in the offshore development industry and writing about them.

Years later, I wanted to test self-publishing a book on Amazon. I'd know about it for a while but never really considered it. But it seemed like a golden opportunity; Amazon is the world's #1 book distributor, owning 70% of the market. Unlike social media giants like Facebook, Pinterest, and YouTube, people go to Amazon with one singular purpose - to **_buy_**. With hundreds of millions of active buyers, with preloaded credit cards, it seemed like the ideal place to publish a book.

So I hired a coach to help me write and market my first book. It was a fitness book and he helped me come up with the hook and title.

I called it *"The Science of Getting Ripped"*.

I did a few key things to make the writing easier; first, I created a rock-solid outline that helped me structure my thoughts. The outline made the actual "writing" incredibly easy.

After I had my outline, I literally dictated my book using an app called Rev.com

I used my outline as a visual guide, and then simply spoke into my phone; almost as if I were giving a talk.

I did this for each chapter. At the end of the process I had 8 audio files that I submitted and got transcribed.

Best of all, they charged $1 per minute and transcribed them within 24 hours.

So I was able to write my book that way within about 2 months. By the time I was ready to sell, I launched it to my email list of 2500 people. When I launched it, I made about $1000.

Now it was a great feeling, but I didn't make much more than that.

Then someone told me to try Facebook advertising to promote my book so I set up Facebook ads to point to my website. The goal was to have people from Facebook come to my site and buy my book.

Sadly, it never worked, but it was a good learning experience. I spent hundreds of dollars getting people to my site, but they ultimately didn't buy.

So there I was, with a book that I had spent over $1000 to create and market. But I barely broke even.

I was so frustrated because I thought this was going to be it. I thought my book would sell and I'd be making tons of passive income again.

But I didn't, so I gave up for a while.

But then, I started taking self-publishing seriously and met a book marketing coach that convinced me to take self-publishing on Amazon seriously.

He had been making money writing and selling fitness books on Amazon Kindle.

I had heard about Amazon Kindle publishing before, but I didn't have the time or energy to think about it.

But now I was intrigued.

He explained his entire process and I started to see the possibility. I put myself in his shoes. I imagined myself doing what he did to successfully launch profitable books.

Then I started taking the steps he laid out in the book.

It took me a few weeks to format my book for Kindle. I could have paid someone on Fiverr to do it, but since it was my first time, I wanted to do it myself.

After that, I launched my book for 99 cents.

First to my email list. It sold over 100 copies.

"Awesome!" I thought to myself.

Amazon only offers a 35% royalty for books that are sold for less than $2.99, so I only made $35 from that promotion to my email list.

But that's ok because those initial sales helped me climb up in the rankings within the Amazon book categories - which made me a bestseller in various categories.

Then I scheduled a bunch of promotions on websites that promote Kindle books.

I'll reveal those sites later in this book, but I staggered them, one day at a time.

By the end of that week, I was a bestseller in multiple categories.

I was so excited!

I was making 15-20 sales per day. That's when I decided to increase my price to $1.99. Then to $2.99.

At that point I was eligible to receive 70% royalties on my book.

It kept selling and selling and selling despite the price increase.

Then I increased it to $3.99 and eventually up to $4.99.

It was an AMAZING feeling to be making nearly $2,000 per month from this book.

A book that I had worked so hard on. And it was pure passive income.

A few months after, I released a paperback version of the book, which I sell for $19.99.

I was hooked on the process, and from that point on, I was DETERMINED to scale this up and write more books and increase my passive income.

That's my crazy, emotional roller coaster of a story on the way to figuring out how to use Amazon to launch a book that earns passive income and boosts my authority.

The beauty of this is that once you sell one book, not only can you replicate the process for other books, you can build a backend business.

I'm talking about video courses, mastermind groups, coaching, seminars, and live events.

This is how millionaires are born.

And it ALL starts with a book.

So, if you're looking for the easiest, fastest, most reliable way to write a book and grow your business, I would have to say that there's been nothing nearly as effective as writing a book and publishing it on Amazon Kindle.

Publishing on Kindle allows you to make money very fast and does NOT require you to know anything about email marketing, web hosting, Wordpress setup, split-testing, SEO, or conversion optimization.

Now coming back to my software development days, just like my blog SoftwareSweatshop.com helped me generate high-value clients, your book is going to help you do the same.

Moral of the Story:

I revealed a lot in this chapter, but the key is that the #1 way to differentiate yourself (next to being featured on reality TV) is to write a book, and use that to establish your presence in the market, exhibit your dominance, and demonstrate your authority.

I'll show you how to do just that with Amazon, LinkedIn, blogs/podcasts, local and national media, industry organizations/associations, and direct outreach to your dream clients.

The goal is to become an elite authorpreneur with a commanding presence in your market that makes it easy to sell your products and services.

Still Not Convinced? (*you will be*)

This next chapter is meant to answer a very simple, but important question.

But before I get to that question, I want to share something that I see over and over and over again. In fact, it's something that I fall victim to myself sometimes as well.

You see, I speak to people over and over again that are excited to write a book, and **<u>know</u>** that it will explode their business.

But after the initial excitement wears off, they fall victim to apathy and doubt and never end up making any progress.

There are a multitude of reasons, from lack of clarity, to not having enough time, to struggling with what to write. As I said, I've fallen victim to these myself multiple times - so I empathize with anyone going through those issues.

But what I've noticed is that behind each of the excuses is a subtle question:

"Is it even worth it to write a book?"

I've said it earlier in this book, but I'll say it again; the answer is unequivocally **_yes_** and I list a few reasons below.

Amazon Handles Printing and Distribution

Often times, I work with clients that have already written and published books. The problem is that they've used traditional publishers and had to not only write the book, they've had to purchase 500-1000 print copies.

It's a painful situation because they end up spending thousands of dollars and then have to figure out how to actually sell the books.

The beauty of publishing on Amazon is that they handle the distribution for you. Recall that Amazon controls 70% of the book market, and if you sell a digital copy of your book, promotion is incredibly simple.

For your Kindle version, you simply upload your manuscript, formatted for Kindle (this is really simple to do). Once you've done that, you can launch your book using the methods I share later in this book.

On top of that, Amazon has the infrastructure and technology to print paperback books "on-demand" meaning you don't need to pre-print hundreds of paperback books and store them in your basement.

Instead, you upload a simple PDF file of your paperback manuscript, and whenever you sell a copy, Amazon prints it on-demand and sends it to the customer.

So take advantage of their infrastructure to launch and promote your book.

Books Require Very Little Up-Front Investment

Do you remember the old adage "it takes money to make money?" Well, that saying also applies online, but not on the same scale. Most businesses require fairly sizeable investments in order for you to start making some serious money.

- I have a friend that spent $250,000 to open a restaurant that eventually failed
- I know another guy that spent hundreds of thousands to open a laundromat
- My parents have invested HUGE amounts of money in their real estate business
- I know people that invested hundreds of thousands of dollars into a software business.

Now all of these businesses could make a lot of money, but they come with a **massive** upfront capital investment.

Books, when compared to many other activities, have nearly no startup costs.

Sure, it does take time and a small investment to publish a book, but it's *a drop in the bucket* compared to starting a traditional brick-and-mortar business.

And if you monetize it right, the income potential could be ***astronomical***.

It's also much, much cheaper than spending tens of thousands of dollars on advertising.

And your book can be used to easily market and promote your book.

Scale Quickly

In the last chapter, we discussed the multiple ways people are making money with their books.

Writing a popular, well-received book is a great way to launch a thriving business.

You can *launch an online course, offer consulting, be invited* (and paid) *to speak to corporations, do live seminars*, and *publish books*.

All from a tiny little book.

Even better, the credibility, connections, and expertise you gain from writing a book can lead to an incredibly strong business in just a few years.

All with very little startup capital or investment (as long as you sell digital products like ebooks, online courses, or software)

Generate Passive Income

One of the main reasons to write a book is because of the massive amount of passive income that it can generate.

As I mentioned earlier in this book, I know of people making tens of thousands of dollars per month by publishing books on a variety of topics. I'm not advocating that method, but I do say it to underscore the potential of generating passive income in the form of revenues.

As you can see below, I make a few thousand dollars per month from my books, and I write about a few different topics - mostly to keep testing what's working in different markets. I do also test various promotional and advertising strategies, so I don't promise that you'll make $5,000 per month from your book, but I do share this as an example of what's possible.

You Can Work From Anywhere in the World

My parents own real estate. I have friends that own restaurants and retail stores. I have a friend that owns a dental practice with his wife.

And they all make a good living.

But the common theme is that they have to be tied down to their business. They either have to provide the service, or manage employees, or otherwise be present at their business.

The beauty of being an authorpreneur is that you can work from anywhere in the world. All you need is electricity, the ability to collect payments, and a reliable internet connection.

I know people that left the US to live in Costa Rica, Bali, India, Thailand, and Mexico and were able to live fun, thrilling lives based on the earnings from their online business.

And a book is the perfect foundation for that.

Books Are Easy To Start

By far the best reason to start a book is that it is extremely easy for anyone to do. One of the major barriers to any business is the large capital investment.

My parents had to invest millions of dollars into their real estate business.

My dentist friend had to invest $1 million dollars into each of his three offices. That includes building the place out and buying dental chairs, dental equipment, x-ray machines, televisions, etc.

I have a friend that lost $250,000 investing in a Middle Eastern restaurant in Miami (*come on bro, rice and hummus won't sell well when everyone is limiting their carbs!*)

I have another friend that's trying to start a software company. He needs $1 million dollars to hire more people and scale up his marketing efforts. He's been looking for investors for nearly 2 years and still hasn't found any.

So the barrier to entry is much, much lower with a book - but if you do it right, it will skyrocket your business.

Own Your Expertise

With self-publishing, the barrier to entry for publishing a book is incredibly low, which means people are publishing books on a near-daily basis.

In some ways this is great, but in other ways, it's a detriment to the industry. Because the barrier to entry is low for a blog doesn't mean that anyone can write a book.

Since you already are an expert, a book is the perfect way to own your expertise and demonstrate your credibility.

You don't necessarily have to be a certified, credentialed, recognized "expert", but you do have to be credible.

That means you have to be a real, authentic person, that helps transform people's lives or businesses, and share your experiences, failures, breakthroughs, and stories in a way that authentically delivers life-changing results.

Key Points:

So, to end this chapter, I want to warn you that being an authorpreneur requires a certain level of mental toughness.

Just like being in any long-term commitment from a marriage to a business partnership, to going to college, you have to be able to work through the fear, doubt, and apathy that most people succumb to after the initial excitement wears off.

So before we go to the next section, I want you to commit to yourself that you're going to make this happen.

THE AUTHORPRENEUR PLEDGE

"I promise that I will do whatever it takes to become an authorpreneur. My business is worth it. My life will be better for it. And I deserve the satisfaction of knowing I accomplished what I set out to do."

SECTION 2

The "RWPPPP" Process

Now that you understand the importance of turning your expertise into a book, and you see the potential of writing a high-quality book, it's time to reveal my RWPPPP (pronounced "rip") framework.

This section contains concise, direct, and powerful descriptions of each step.

I see a TON of people writing books, but most of them have NO idea how to promote it. They literally spend 12 months writing, pouring their heart and soul into it, only to be met with crickets.

It's *incredibly* depressing.

If you follow these steps, you **_will_** become a bestseller on Amazon. And if you follow the steps in Section 3 of this book, you'll be able to capitalize on that success and really build a profitable business.

Quick Story:

I wrote a book a few years ago and STRUGGLED to sell it.

I tried EVERYTHING from blogging to Facebook ads, to YouTube — but it was an utter failure.

I even got my Facebook ad account banned (long story...)

Then, a mentor convinced me to publish it on Amazon.

I was skeptical, but I figured I didn't have anything to lose.

Luckily, I already had the book, and I created a really compelling title, subtitle, and cover - so I was hopeful that it would do well.

A few days later I uploaded it on Amazon (*this part is a piece of cake*)

Then, I followed a specific system to launch it, and within a week it became an instant bestseller.

That first month I made $1800 on complete autopilot and it was an amazing feeling.

Now, I've developed a simple and repeatable method to earn more income (I make $3k-$5k a month), build my list of leads, and sell coaching and consulting services - that all have the potential to make MUCH more.

Over the years, I created a simple framework and called it my "RWPPPP" (pronounced "rip") framework. It stands for:

Research

Write

Position

Publish

Profit

Promote

If you follow this system, you can consistently create profitable books that you can use to earn royalties, build your email list, and launch lucrative online courses, coaching, consulting, and paid speaking.

Let's dive in...

Research *(the <u>most</u> underestimated step)*

When it comes to business, I have 4 simple mantras:

"Mimic what works"

"Model success"

"Find a hungry audience"

"Fish where the fish are, but use the right bait"

That simply means we want to do what's working (*no need to reinvent the wheel, right?*)

That means we want to research Amazon to see what's already selling. This is my **<u>most</u>** VALUABLE secret. You've got to see what people are already buying and simply model that.

People go to Amazon to do one thing; <u>*to buy stuff*</u>. So if something's selling well on Amazon, we want to simply model that. (*and make it better of course*)

Amazon has TONS of traffic; hundreds of millions of buyers with preloaded credit cards who are looking to **buy.**

The **KEY** is to give people what they're already buying.

We do that by looking at what's already selling on Amazon.

Then you simply position your book within categories that are already selling well.

This is the **biggest** difference between books that succeed and books that flop.

You want to write books in categories where the books have good ABSR (Amazon Best Seller Rank).

Understanding bestseller rank is the **#1** way to determine the profitability of a topic. The lower your ABSR is, the more you will sell.

You want to rank your book as a #1 bestseller in multiple categories, this gives you **exposure** from multiple categories and subcategories.

- Certain categories have a LOT of interest:

- **Fiction**:
  - Erotica
  - Romance
  - Mystery
  - Suspense
- **Non-Fiction**
  - Business & Money (tech, communication, leadership, social media, etc.)
  - Self Help (motivation, mindfulness, anxiety, personal development, etc.)
  - Spirituality (religion, inspirational, meditation, etc.)
  - Relationships (marriage, parenting, etc.)
  - Health & Fitness (diet, weight loss, muscle building, wellness, etc.)
  - Cookbooks
  - History

The key is to look at the categories that you want to write about - chances are you can fit your topic into one of the categories above. Even if your topic isn't *directly* related to one of the categories above, you can position it in a way via your title and subtitle that allows you to position yourself into one of those lucrative categories.

And that comes down to deeply understanding your ideal customer's deeply held desires, fears, and struggles but we'll get to that later.

As for evaluating the competitive landscape, I want the #5 bestselling book in my categories to be ranked 30,000 or below. That tells me it's selling well, but that I also have a shot of hitting the top 5 also.

On average, ABSR of 30000 means the book is making $300-$500 per month (assuming it's selling for $2.99)

It probably makes twice that amount if there's a paperback and audiobook version.

If the average ABSR is 5000-10000 for the first 20 bestselling books, I'll go for it. If the top 5 books are below 5000 and the rest are much lower, I'll go for it.

The beauty of this system is that Amazon tells you how well books are selling (see images below). If you see that the bestselling books in certain categories have an ABSR of 5000-10000, that tells you that you've found a profitable category where people are buying and the competition is low enough so that you can actually compete and rank your book highly - if you position it properly and launch it aggressively.

Once I've found a profitable category for my book, I'll research 5-10 other categories that are relevant to my book because I want as much exposure as possible by placing my book in as many categories and subcategories as possible.

The trick is to find very niche categories that you can **dominate** so that you become a bestseller.

When that happens, people will be more inclined to buy, which will increase your sales rank, allowing you to switch your book into more competitive categories.

From my personal experience, if you can sell **just 15 copies of a book per day**, you can become a bestseller.

Look at the screenshots below to see what I mean.

Amazon Best Sellers
Our most popular products based on sales. Updated hourly

- Any Department
- Kindle Store
- Kindle eBooks
- Health, Fitness & Dieting
  - Counseling & Psychology
  - Adolescent Psychology
  - Applied Psychology
  - Child Psychology
  - Clinical Psychology
  - Cognitive Neuroscience & Cognitive Neuropsychology
  - Counseling
  - Creativity & Genius
  - Developmental Psychology
  - **Education & Training** ← Niche category
  - Ethnopsychology
  - Experimental Psychology
  - Forensic Psychology
  - Grief & Loss
  - Group Therapy
  - History
  - Hypnosis
  - Medicine & Psychology
  - Mental Health
  - Movements
  - Neuropsychology
  - Occupational & Organizational
  - Pathologies
  - Personality
  - Physiological Aspects
  - Practice Management
  - Psychoanalysis
  - Psychopharmacology
  - Psychotherapy, TA & NLP
  - Reference
  - Research
  - Sexuality

Best Sellers in **Psychology Education & Training**

Top 100 Paid   Top 100 Free

1.
Man's Search for Meaning
- Viktor E. Frankl
★★★★☆ 3,443
Kindle Edition
$9.99

2.
The Fearless Mind
- Craig Manning
★★★★☆ 50
Kindle Edition
$3.99

3.
15 Secrets Successf...
- Kevin Kruse
★★★★☆ 330
Kindle Edition
$4.99

4.
Peak: Secrets from the...
- Anders Ericsson
★★★★☆ 186
Kindle Edition
$14.99

5. kindleunlimited

Learn: Cognitive...
- Sebastian Archer
★★★★☆ 28
Kindle Edition
$2.99

6. kindleunlimited

Summary - The Pow...
EZ-Summary
★★★★★ 4
Kindle Edition
$2.99

7. (Conversation Tactics)

8. kindleunlimited

9. kindleunlimited

Hunting for categories is **<u>crucial</u>** – as you sell more copies, you can move into more competitive categories.

Just like ranking your website in Google for certain keywords, the crux of my entire strategy is to hunt for categories that I can easily rank highly in so that I can become a bestseller, generating even more organic sales.

Once you're a bestseller in your categories, have good reviews, and have had multiple days of strong sales, you can increase your price and really start profiting.

As for research, I usually research a few critical items:

- **Research Competitors**: Your title and subtitle are some of the MOST important factors to selling your book, so pay close attention to the titles and subtitles of other books that are selling in your target categories. Look at the titles of the bestsellers in your niche:
    - Are there common themes?
    - Do they use **alliteration**?
    - Are the titles **clear**, **concise**, and **compelling**?
    - Do they call out a **specific** audience?

- Do they address a **<u>specific</u>** problem?
- Do the titles imply a **<u>benefit</u>** to the reader?
- Do they convey **emotion**?
- **Backend Offer**: Do they have a link in the book that directs the user to join their email list? If so, what product or service are they offering their readers inside the book?
  - Paid speaking
  - Corporate consulting
  - Coaching
  - Courses
- **Other Books**: Does the author have other books?
  - How many other books do they have?
  - What other topics do they write about?
  - How well are they selling?
- **Web Presence**: Do they have the following:
  - Blog
  - Podcast
  - YouTube channel
  - Facebook groups

- LinkedIn presence
- **Average Page Length:** Look at the **average** page length of books that are similar to yours
- Short vs Long:
    - A short, 50, 75, or 150 page book that focuses on a specific topic will generally sell **better** than longer books because people want **quick**, **easy**, **simple**, and **brief**
    - Be sure to include **stories**, **emotion**, **ups and downs**, **obstacles**, **breakthroughs**, **tips**, **tricks**, and **hacks**
- **Positive Reviews**: Read what people love and make sure that your book incorporates those points. Things people love:
    - Simplicity
    - Stories
    - Brevity and conciseness
    - Relatability
    - Step-by-step instructions

- **Negative Reviews**: <u>Read what readers hate about the book </u>(this is your opportunity to **shine**) Common complaints in negative reviews include:
    - Repetitiveness in the book
    - Too much theory and not enough practical advice
    - Poor spelling and grammar
    - Rehashing old material
- **Book Covers**: Your book cover is arguably the **#1** factor that will cause your book to sell, so pay close attention to bestselling book covers in your genre
    - **Simplicity**: I find that **simple** covers do the best. Look at the bestseller list in the business, health/fitness, self-help categories.
    - **Colors**: I find that **<u>stark color contrast</u>** works really well. Or simple white backgrounds with dark text
    - **Images**: Non-fiction books should use images very **<u>sparsely</u>**. If used, they

should accentuate and compliment that title and subtitle, **NOT** overpower them
- **Self-Published vs Publishing House**: You want to check to see if the book is self-published or published via a publishing house
    - **Promotions:**
        - Publishing houses have lots of money to invest in promotions, this makes it harder for you to compete
        - If you see lots of self-published books, you know that you have more of a chance to succeed
    - **Pricing**: On the other hand, publishing houses price their books much higher. This is good for you
- Pricing Matters:
    - 99 cents is a typical price for launching your Kindle book
    - Most self-published books sell for $2.99 after the initial launch

- Big publishers price their books much higher ($9.99 to $19.99)

As you can see, you want to spend a lot of time researching books that are already selling well in your target categories, because if you can understand <u>*why*</u> they're selling so well, you'll have much better chances of publishing a book that does just as well.

The point is that you have to write about something that people care about.

And Amazon is **<u>amazing</u>** for telling you what people care about.

The way to do that is to browse the bestseller categories (and subcategories) and see what's selling.

Look at the covers.

Look at the titles.

Look at the descriptions.

Look at the reviews.

The **<u>last</u>** thing you want to do is write something that nobody wants.

Luckily, with Amazon, you can see what's selling in real-time and make sure that your book incorporates some of those elements.

Now, simply identify at least 5 books that are in your niche that are selling well.

By "well" I mean that their ABSR is 100,000 or lower. If you find books like that then you know that people are interested in that topic. It also means that you have a chance to actually compete.

Writing *(how to write an awesome non-fiction book in 24 hours)*

I had the idea to write one of my books back in 2016 but waited for a year and a half to finally "have time" to write it.

When I decided that enough was enough, I got it done; *in less than a month*.

So my advice to you is this; **don't procrastinate**, just get the book done.

The best part is that you can do it relatively quickly if you have a solid plan.

My **#1 secret** is to have a solid outline. An outline relieves the mental stress of having to write a book and allows you to easily map out your thoughts.

As for an outline, you want to come up with 7-10 chapter names, then write 3 sub-chapters, and for each sub-chapter, write 3 main points.

The beauty of this process is that it allows you to see everything at once, which will generate more and more ideas.

Here's how your outline should look:

Chapter 1

Subchapter 1

-main point 1

-main point 2

-main point 3

Subchapter 2

-main point 1

-main point 2

-main point 3

Subchapter 3

-main point 1

-main point 2

-main point 3

Chapter 2 (do the same as above)

Can you see how you're starting to put together the structure of your book very easily, systematically, and methodically?

In fact, there's a great free software online called MindMup.com

It really helps you visualize the entire book.

You can drill down further and further to structure your thought process.

The beauty of this process is that it allows you to see everything at once, which will generate more and more ideas.

Then it's simply a matter of dumping every **story**, **fact**, **lesson**, **breakthrough**, **epiphany**, **personal experience**, **struggle**, and **idea** that you can into the outline.

Heart-pounding, suspenseful, full of drama, mystery, and intrigue; we aren't talking about the latest John Grisham book, I'm talking about your personal story.

It's called "The Hero's Journey" and it's a tried and true formula of every blockbuster Hollywood film.

There's something magical that happens when we follow a person on their personal journey of transformation. We see them start confused, scared, unsure of themselves, and then step into their power and turn into a hero.

It's a tried-and-true formula that bestselling fiction authors and Hollywood scriptwriters use to hook their audience and build emotional resonance. Just look at this list:

- The Wizard of Oz
- Harry Potter
- The Karate Kid
- The Matrix
- Terminator 2
- The Last Samurai
- The Notebook
- Breaking Bad
- Forrest Gump
- Gladiator

Like I've said earlier in this book, your book needs to contain these 3 critical elements:

- Story
- Emotion
- Imagery

People won't remember the dry "how-to" information you're teaching. But they **_will_** remember the emotions that you made them feel. You want them to feel the fear, frustration, and eventual joy that you felt along your journey. You want to wrap you "how-to" content into a story so that they feel every disappointment, breakthrough, discovery, struggle, and "aha moment" you felt.

You want to use imagery and share specific details so that it paints a picture in your reader's mind.

So focus on personal stories or case studies of work that you've done with past clients.

Remember, ***facts tell, stories sell***

That's what I did for my very first book, *The Science of Getting Ripped*.

I documented exactly how I got in shape. I even searched articles from big websites and copied and pasted the main points into my outline (weight lifting, calories/macros, benefits of high-intensity cardio, etc.)

I then **rewrote** it to fit my experiences, share my struggles, etc. This helped get my creative juices flowing so I could start expanding on the point myself.

If you're struggling to write, here's a brief meditation that I use when I'm struggling... and like magic, I **suddenly** feel **inspired**, **creative**, **motivated**, **confident**, and **optimistic**.

You should find it helpful:

I want you to close your eyes and breathe deeply. Get into a calm, peaceful, meditative state... and then speak to yourself in an empowering tone. Say something like:

"I know exactly what I want to say in this chapter. I know exactly what I want my reader to learn in this chapter. I know exactly what I want my reader to feel after reading this chapter. I know exactly what result I

want my reader to have after reading this chapter. I want to use my own story, journey, experiences, insights, struggles, and lessons to transform my reader.

I want my reader to learn A, B, and C after reading this chapter.

Before reading this chapter, my reader feels lost, uncertain, and is looking for answers. After reading this chapter, I want my reader to leave feeling XYZ way because I shared _____ lesson/experience/story.

I want my reader to have Z result that they can achieve after reading this chapter."

By doing this, you are **triggering your subconscious mind** to take over. You're moving out of a state of helplessness and frustration (writer's block), and moving into a state of **creativity** and **inner-genius** by talking to yourself in a strong, positive, confident way. When you do this, you'll ***feel*** a surge of inspiration because you're **activating** your subconscious mind and **unlocking** the genius within you.

Once you get that feeling, you'll notice a flood of ideas coming to you. To keep them structured, I want you to add just one of the following to each sub-point in your chapter:

- **Mention Top Problems:** If you haven't already, mention specific **problems**, **pain points**, **issues**, or **concerns** that are related to your chapter/sub-point. Starting with the main problems helps build empathy with the reader and also frames the rest of the chapter to *solve* the problem, which keeps the reader's interest.

- **Share Personal Stories**: Something you've personally experienced. Retell the experience, how you felt, what people were saying to you, the outcome, and the lesson you learned.

- **Mention Research/Facts**: If you don't have any stories about that part, mention any research, facts, or common industry knowledge on the topic. Often times, you can go to Inc Magazine, Business Insider, Harvard Business Review, etc. and find something related to your sub-point. Then, just simply cite the article, research, study, fact, etc.

- **Techniques**: Share a specific **technique**, **tool**, **method**, **formula**, or **process** you've used to solve a specific problem related to the chapter.

3 Ways to TURBOCHARGE Your Writing Results

Now that you have your chapters, your sub-chapters, and your three main points under each sub-chapter written, the next thing for you to do is to start writing the body content.

Method #1: Dictating Your Book:

This is how I got my first book written in a matter of weeks. In fact, a majority of my time was spent creating my outline, gathering my material, and editing. The actual "writing" took a few days because I dictated my audio files into my phone and had them transcribed.

I didn't have a lot of time to sit down and write, but after I had my outline and my sub-chapters and my main points under my sub-chapters, all I had to do was pick up my iPhone, turn on the voice recording app, and start speaking out what I wanted to write.

Once I had that, I was able to submit it to a voice-to-text transcribing company (I recommend Temi.com)

Transcribing your books is amazing and a complete game-changer.

Method #2: Write in Short Sentences

Another absolute game changer is how you write.

If you notice, I write in short paragraphs.

Each paragraph is only one or two sentences.

This is on purpose.

When I write that way, I feel more conversational.

I'm able to see the words that I've just written, and I can then build upon them very quickly.

Almost like I'm having a conversation with a friend.

Using this method, I can easily write 1000 words in less than an hour.

Sometimes I can write close to 2000 words.

At this pace, I can get a 20,000-word draft written in 10 days.

Method #3: Hire a Ghostwriter:

Another option is to get it written by a ghostwriter.

But, I DON'T recommend that you have a ghostwriter create a low quality book that you slap your name on.

If you use a ghostwriter, be sure to put your own spin on the book.

Have a unique angle.

Add your own story.

No matter how you write the book, you need to edit it for content and grammar.

I've skipped this step in previous books and it's resulted in negative reviews on Amazon.

Whether you write the book yourself, dictate it, or hire a ghostwriter, just choose one and get the book done. My books are anywhere between 75–125 pages long and I can write them in about a month if I'm focused.

So over the next 5 days, I want you to do the following:

1. **Outline**: Create an outline
2. **Write**: Get the book done
   - Spend 1 hour a day writing or dictating the book
   - Do this every day for 10 days
   - Aim for 2000 words per session
     - It's easier than you think ***if*** you have an outline
3. **Edit**: The first version will need to be edited:
   - Friends/family
   - Professional editor on UpWork

Sit down and start writing your outline.

Just get it done because once you do, writing the entire book will seem way less daunting.

After that, you should write for one hour a day.

If you can write 1000-2000 words per session, you'll have the book done in 10-15 days.

Open your phone and start dictating your book. You can choose to type it out as well, but if you have very little time, dictating will help tremendously.

I prefer Rev.com, because they're very fast and accurate, but it's totally up to you.

Just think about that for a second. Let's say that you dictate into your phone for 60 minutes. You simply pay $60 and you have the makings of your next bestselling book.

It's absolutely amazing, and at that pace, you can write a book in 24 hours, but it all comes back down to having a solid outline, sub-chapters, and main points under your sub-chapters.

Try to write your book in just 10 days. I know it sounds _crazy,_ but it's **doable** if you're focused. Spend just 1 hour per day (25 wpm = 1500 wph)

Don't make it more complicated than it is.

I wrote the **Passive Income Playbook** in just under 3 weeks; but I put it off for over 1.5 years. I wrote in the morning, when my kids napped, late at night, during lunch at my job

That book has made me tens of thousands of dollars, so it's WORTH IT!

Positioning *(how to blow your competition out of the water)*

This is where you take all of the research you did in step one to create an engaging, thought-provoking, curiosity-inducing title, subtitle, and cover that makes your readers <u>*eager*</u> to buy.

Imagine you want to open a food truck and sell on the beach.

There are tons of people there so you figure it makes sense to go there.

It's probably a hot day. People are playing volleyball, they're rollerblading, they're swimming, they're walking on the hot sand...

Now imagine trying to sell them hot chocolate instead of ice cream!

If you don't do your research and notice what they're already buying - your business will flop.

And that's the #1 reason I see people failing with their books.

That's why research matters; it helps you **position** your book so you give people exactly what they want.

I keep speaking to clients that spend the time to write a book but don't take the time to research the market and position their book to actually make money.

That's why this chapter is so important...

When it comes to selling your book, the 3 most important elements are:

1. A **COMPELLING** title that addresses what your audience wants
2. A **KILLER** cover that gets their attention
3. An **AGGRESSIVE** launch plan that makes your audience aware of you

In this chapter, you'll discover how to do the first two...

Remember, you can have the best book in the world, but if no one buys it, you'll never make money from it.

Your hook/title should be:

- Unique
- Attention-grabbing
- Address an emotional need
- Solve a BIG problem
- Allude to a solution
- Convey something cool, amazing, and earth-shattering

So you HAVE to think of a hook.

The hook is even more important than the actual content if you want to sell.

Because you're going to use your hook in the title and subtitle.

And top copywriters will tell you that they spend 80% of their time writing a good headline.

That's how important your hook/headline/title is.

Because if a browser looks at your title and isn't interested, he or she will just move on and never buy your book.

Of course, the content HAS to be good, but if you ignore the hook, no one will buy it.

Make it emotional.

Make it gripping.

Make it powerful.

I went through multiple iterations of my title when I first wrote my book. Take a look and think about which one resonates the most with you:

- First Title:
  - **Inner Strength, Functional Physique (BAD)**
- Second Title:
  - **The Lean Muscle Secret**: How to Get Ripped in 90 Days (BETTER)
- Third Title:
  - **The Science of Getting Ripped**: Proven Workout Tricks and Diet Hacks

to Build Muscle and Burn Fat in Half the Time (WINNER)

Here's why it worked: it had a catchy title. It used copywriting power words "hack" and "tricks". It made a promise. And it made it time specific.

Spending time writing a good title is so important because the title is going to grab the reader's attention and spark their curiosity.

As for writing titles, it helps to look at other bestselling titles to generate ideas. I've included some of my favorites below:

Switch

No Easy Day

Thug Kitchen

Skinny Bitch

Skinny Bitch in the Kitch

How to Win Friends and Influence People

Deep Work

The One Thing

The Blue Ocean Strategy

Rich Dad, Poor Dad

The Art of the Deal

The Millionaire Next Door

The Four Hour Work Week

The Subtle Art of Not Giving a F*ck

The Life-Changing Magic of Tidying Up

The 7 Habits of Highly Effective People

How to Think Like a Spy

Freakonomics

Looking at other great titles is an awesome way to come up with new ideas for your own title. Remember, we want to model what's already working and identify common themes that we can incorporate into our own titles.

As for writing titles, here's what I recommend:

- Write out 15-20 (most will be bad, but this will get the creative process going)
- Call out a **specific** audience demographic

- Address a **specific pain** the reader is experiencing
- Describe the **benefits** the reader will get by reading the book
- Make a **specific promise** to the reader - promise a desirable end result or outcome

You also want to incorporate the following "**power**" words into your title and subtitle:

- "How to"
- "Practical"
- "Proven"
- "Guide"
- "Your"
- "Simple"
- "Step-by-Step"
- "Secrets"
- "Hacks"
- "Formula"

- "Process"
- "Fastest"
- "Method"
- "Blueprint"
- "Easiest"
- "Foolproof"
- "Even If..."
- "Without"

Now that we've covered the title and subtitle of your book, we want to focus on the cover.

For non-fiction books, you'll notice that some of the bestselling books of all time have a few common elements. They are clean, direct, simple, and use large, bold text with stark color contrasts.

Malcolm Gladwell, Michael Lewis, Jim Collins, and James Clear have amazing covers built on these same principles.

Below are examples of some of my favorite non-fiction book covers:

GREAT Non-Fiction Covers

As for actually creating your covers, I recommend 3 options:

- **Fiverr:**
    - **Pros**: Very cost effective
    - **Cons**: You need to be very specific; purchase unlimited revisions
- **99Designs:**
    - **Pros**: You'll get lots of designs from multiple designers
    - **Cons**: Most expensive
- **Canva:**
    - **Pros**: They have great templates and

it's very cost effective
- ○ **Cons**: You need to take some time to tweak them

Whichever you choose, you'll probably need to make revisions and go through multiple iterations until you feel it's perfect - so be sure to plan for that.

The next thing is to choose great categories to position your book in. This is VITALLY important because you want to become a bestseller in less competitive categories during your launch - this will **boost your exposure** and organic sales.

As I mentioned in the "research" section of this book, list out 10 categories that you want your book to be in. Try to put them in multiple parent categories to double your exposure.

For example, if you're writing a paleo cookbook, put it in the "Cookbooks" and "Health and Fitness" categories, and related subcategories. If you write about personal development/focus/productivity, put it under the "Self Help" and "Business and Money" categories.

Now that you've positioned your book in relevant categories that you can dominate, you want to focus on keywords. In my opinion, dominating categories on Amazon Kindle is more important than ranking for keywords, so I don't pay too much attention to keywords, but they're still important.

I've found that the **<u>EASIEST</u>** way to find keywords is to use Amazon auto-suggest. Just type a few keywords slowly in the Amazon search bar and see what auto-suggested keywords appear - you're basically using Amazon to tell you what keywords are popular.

Lastly, you want to write a really good description. As for descriptions, the age old copywriting adage goes:

"Sell the sizzle, not the steak"

Here, you want to focus on 3 things:

- **Emotion:** Describe the problem and incite their emotions
- **Story:** Tell a story of how you struggled

- **Imagery:** Paint a picture of what life will be like once they buy your book and follow your system

Another Framework:

- **Problem**: Describe the problem in detail, make it emotional
- **Agitate**: Agitate the problem by describing the consequences to the reader
- **Solution**: Allude to a solution, and paint a picture of how life will be better

To summarize, you want to start positioning your book ***before*** it's ready... that way when the book is done you'll be all set.

Here's a quick recap of what to work on as you think about your positioning:

1. **Title**: You need to have a really catchy title and subtitle. It's got to be emotional, hit on a pain point, and imply ease (blueprint, system, method, framework, step-by-step, etc.) Write out 15-20 titles and choose the best ones
2. **Cover**: Simple, bold covers do best. Study the bestselling books and pay attention to what

their covers look like.

3. **Description**: Use my templates to write a sizzling description for your book
4. **Categories**: Choose 10 categories and subcategories that you can place your book in. You want the average Amazon Bestseller Rank of the books in your target subcategories to be around 30,000 - that means that you can easily outrank them and become a bestseller.
5. **Keywords**: Look for 7 keywords that are related to your book
6. **Number of Pages**: Your book can be as short as 75 pages the important thing is to provide a quick, easy, simple solution to their problems.

Profit on Backend *(this is where the <u>real</u> money is made)*

In this section I'll show you how to make <u>10X</u> more money from your backend profit system.

- Overview of your backend system

- How to get **<u>eager</u>** prospects to contact YOU

- What you can offer to them to make **<u>10X</u>** more money

Think about musicians; they make <u>a few cents per dollar</u> from each CD they sell; their ***real*** money comes from concerts, merchandise, etc.

Your book can definitely make hundreds and even thousands per month in book royalties (I make $3k to $7k per month in book royalties and know people that make up to $20k per month in royalties alone), but you're leaving ***<u>MASSIVE</u>*** amounts of money on the table if you don't have a backend profit strategy.

Here's how you can literally make tens of thousands per month from your book in backend services:

1. **Coaching:** I've made **<u>thousands of dollars</u>** offering my coaching services. People read my book and then contact me to coach them.
2. **Consulting:** This is similar to coaching, except businesses actually have hired me to consult for them after reading my books.
3. **Speaking:** People make tens of thousands of dollars speaking to corporations; this is an absolute goldmine if you can speak to executives at large corporations
4. **Online Courses:** I've made thousands of dollars from my online courses and know of people that make 6-figures from people that buy their books and then buy their online courses

You just have to make it easy for your customers to contact you. *I've personally made thousands and thousands of dollars in coaching and course sales by connecting with my audience and <u>giving them what they want.</u>*

Here's how:

Offer some kind of lead magnet in your book. A lead magnet is a piece of content that you offer for free in exchange for an email address so that you can continue to communicate with them.

Here are a few good examples:

- Cheat Sheets
- 1-Page Checklists
- Free Reports
- Audiobook
- Videos
- Etc.

It doesn't have to be huge it just needs to solve a **<u>specific</u>** problem that people have. Here a few of my top converting lead magnets. I simply mention them in the beginning and end of my books and have gotten up to 30+ new email subscribers per day from my books:

- The Dessert Report (a few pages)
- 60 Seconds of Focus (one pager)

- The Passive Income Playbook Cheat Sheet (11 pages)

These are short, easy to create, very direct, and actionable.

As a result, I have people contacting me for coaching consistently.

Remember, people that have bought your book are some of the most qualified prospects for your services. They've already spent money on your book and they know that you're the real deal. Most likely, they want the quickest, easiest, fastest solution to their problem - and they'll be willing to pay you for it.

If nothing else, just leave your email address and/or phone number and invite people to contact you

I know of an author that has made $250k from a simple little call to action in the top of his employee engagement book.

He speaks to corporations on how they can improve their employee engagement and charges $12k to $15k to speak to executives on the topic.

How did he get those companies to contact him? A simple little note at the beginning of his book.

To recap, you **will** make money from selling the book, but the real money is made on the backend. The real trick is to have people contact you for other products and services.

Powerful stuff here's a screenshot of $7,000 in course sales and coaching I earned in one month:

AuthorPreneur Elite

All	Draft	Unpaid	**Paid**

0039 – Paid — $697.00 — Sep 18, 2018

0038 – Paid — $697.00 — Sep 15, 2018

0036 – Paid — $697.00 — Sep 13, 2018

0035 – Paid — $697.00 — Sep 12, 2018

0034 – Paid — $697.00 — Sep 11, 2018

0033 – Paid — $2,000.00 — Sep 1, 2018

0032 – Paid — $1,500.00 — Jul 18, 2018

Publish *(bring your book to <u>life</u>)*

If you've done everything I told you to this point, you should be ready to publish; so I created a **<u>simple</u>** checklist to make sure your book is ready to launch.

It's time to celebrate because you're **<u>almost</u>** there do this and you'll be ready to launch!

1. **Create GREAT Content**: Your book should be **<u>clear</u>**, **<u>concise</u>**, **<u>have stories</u>**, **<u>share tips</u>**, **<u>have insights</u>**, **<u>share your failures</u>**, **<u>struggles</u>**, **<u>defeats</u>**, as well as **<u>accomplishments</u>**, **<u>discoveries</u>**, and **<u>breakthroughs.</u>** The end goal is a 75-150 page book that you can be **<u>proud</u>** of
2. **Catchy Title, Subtitle, and Chapter Titles:** You should already have your book title and subtitle:
    - Additionally, each chapter should have a **<u>descriptive</u>**, **<u>catchy</u>**, **<u>benefit laden</u>**,

- **curiosity inducing** titles (just look at the module names of this course!)
- Popular authors like Tony Robbins, Malcolm Gladwell, Stephen Dubner and Steven Levitt of Freakonomics all do this really well.

3. **Call to Action to Other Services**:
   - Have a link to an optin form at the beginning and end of your book - ***or better yet***, just your email address so people can contact you.
   - Remember, the book earns royalties, but when they contact you for additional services is when you make the ***real*** money

4. **Pay Attention to the First 10%**:
   - The first 10% of your book should hook the reader, build curiosity, and entice them to buy.
   - Since Amazon allows browsers to preview the first 10% of the book, you **REALLY** want to put some great value here.

- That's why I tell you to create catchy chapter titles (so it creates curiosity) and to have a way for them to contact you, that way they can visit your site or email you even if they don't buy the book

5. **Ask for Reviews:**
    - At the end of the book be **SURE** to ask for reviews
        - Most people will forget if you don't ask so be sure to include a page that asks for a kind and honest review
    - Ask for friends and family for reviews so you can add them as editorial reviews on Amazon Author Central

6. **Edit Again:**
    - I've gotten some bad reviews because my editing wasn't 100% because I accidentally uploaded a version that wasn't edited well so make sure it's edited well
    - **Top reasons** you'll get bad reviews:
        - Poor grammar

- Repetitiveness
- Lack of actionable content
- Oversimplifying things (be sure to add stories to make it more believable)

7. **Write a GREAT Description:**
   - The best way to do this is to look at **OTHER** book descriptions of books in your genre and model (don't copy) them.
   - Pay attention to:
     - Headline
     - Bullet points they use (often times this will be the chapter names),
     - Calls to action

8. **Choose Keywords:**
   - Choose keywords based on what your audience is searching for on Amazon; remember, Amazon auto-suggest is your friend

9. **Format for Ebook and Paperback:**
   - I almost **always** pay someone to do the formatting for me.

- You can pay people on Fiverr to format the Kindle and paperback versions for you. If you go on Fiverr and search "paperback formatting" and "Kindle formatting" you'll find a lot of people who will do that for you. Be sure to ask for:
  - Clickable table of contents
  - Proper margins for paperback
  - Paperback cover with spine and description on back

10. **Create an Audiobook:**
- To increase royalties, you want to have an audiobook created. You can simply go to ACX.com and either:
  - **Pay**: Pay a few hundred dollars to have a professional narrator record your book
  - **Partner**: Partner with someone to record your book and split the royalties with them (I've chosen this one to save money on the front end)

11. **Publish:**

- Go through actually publishing the book on kdp.amazon.com. It's really easy if you've done all of the work above, just simply upload it

  ○ Kindle version

  ○ Paperback version

  ○ Audiobook version (on ACX.com)

You're almost ready to launch and promote your book!

Promotion *(launch like a Hollywood <u>blockbuster</u>)*

Here's what we're going to cover in this section:

- My **<u>super simple</u>** launch plan to make sure your book becomes a bestseller

- **<u>Paid vs. Free</u>** book launch strategy

- The **<u>perfect</u>** price to launch your book

- The **<u>best</u>** places to promote your book

- How to ensure **<u>ongoing</u>** sales after your launch

Think about how Hollywood produces and promotes movies they build a LOT of buzz during launch phase:

- Trailers before other movies

- TV commercials

- Web ads

- Billboards

- Media appearances/interviews
- Pre-release screenings
- Film festivals

To summarize, they launch aggressively.

I've been able to generate multiple bestsellers by creating aggressive launch plans - and you can do the same.

If you spent the time to research your market and position your book properly (strong title, attractive cover, great chapter names, telling stories and using emotion in your writing), you'll be able to ride the wave and continue to sell very well after your initial launch.

Another book of mine:

File Size: 2368 KB
Print Length: 100 pages
Simultaneous Device Usage: Unlimited
Publication Date: March 6, 2018
Sold by: Amazon Digital Services LLC
Language: English
ASIN: B07B8XH9CR
Text-to-Speech: Enabled
X-Ray: Not Enabled
Word Wise: Enabled
Lending: Enabled
Screen Reader: Supported
Enhanced Typesetting: Enabled
Amazon Best Sellers Rank: #707 Paid in Kindle Store (See Top 100 Paid in Kindle Store)
  #1 in Books > Business & Money > Small Business & Entrepreneurship > **Marketing**
  #1 in Books > Business & Money > Marketing & Sales > **Advertising**
  #1 in Books > Business & Money > Skills > **Business Writing**

The goal is to launch **AGGRESSIVELY** and **CONSISTENTLY** generate sales. This will show Amazon that your book is selling on its own... once that happens, they'll start to *promote you themselves*.

And believe me, that's a **<u>beautiful</u>** thing!

I end up spending $500-$1000 to launch my books, but **<u>the money comes back to me 2X</u>** because I get email subscribers and get listed as a bestseller, which generates even more sales.

The most successful authors on Amazon spend around the same.

As for launching, a popular strategy is to set the price to free and try to generate as many free downloads as possible, but I don't like that strategy as much.

Below is a screenshot of a free promo that I did. As you can see I generated a LOT of downloads.

And I got ranked REALLY highly in the free store:

Amazon Best Sellers Rank: #12 Free in Kindle Store (See Top 100 Free in Kindle Store)
  #1 in Kindle Store > Kindle Short Reads > Two hours or more (65-100 pages) > **Cookbooks, Food & Wine**
  #1 in Kindle Store > Kindle eBooks > Cookbooks, Food & Wine > **Quick & Easy**

I got over 7,000 free downloads of that book in one day, but when I switched it to a paid book, it dropped like a rock and I didn't make any sales. I barely got any email subscribers from all of those free downloads of the book either.

My theory is that people download free books on Amazon but never get around to actually reading them.

Bottom Line: I **don't** recommend launching your book for free if you want to make money from it...

Here's what I recommend for a launch:

- Price your book at $0.99 so it gets the MOST amount of sales possible (you'll only get 35% royalties at this price)
- Having a paperback (priced at $14.99) and an audiobook is so important because you'll recoup your money from audiobook and paperback sales
- DON'T expect to make money during the launch
    - The goal is to become a bestseller in multiple categories

- Show Amazon that you can consistently drive sales to your book
- Get lots of reviews (aim for 10)
- THEN Amazon will start to promote you
- People will find you on the bestseller lists

If you do it right, you can generate dozens (even hundreds of sales) at 99 cents, which will cause you to become a bestseller in multiple categories. Then you can increase the price to $2.99.

Here's how it should look.

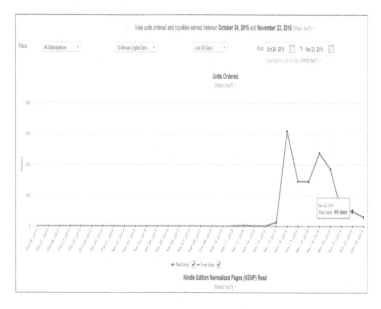

As for promoting the book, there are dozens of websites that promote discounted Kindle books to their email subscribers. These sites have tens of thousands (and even hundreds of thousands of email subscribers that are hungry for discounted books)

The beauty is that you can pay them to promote your book to their email subscribers!

That's the **_secret_** strategy I use to generate tons of sales consistently. The idea is to stagger your promotions so that you generate sales consistently for 1-2 weeks; this is enough to "train" the Amazon algorithm and show them that your book is popular, at which point Amazon starts promoting you...

And believe me, it's **_awesome_** what that happens!

Below is the exact launch plan I use, as well as the websites that deliver the most amount of sales for me:

Day 1:

- Promote to your email, Facebook, LinkedIn, etc. (tell them it's only 99 cents for 1-week and that you'd LOVE if they bought and left a review)
- BKnight on Fiverr

- BookRaid.com (click the "Promote a Book" link at the bottom)

Day 2:

- BargainBooksy
- BookBongo.com
- EbookHounds.com
- eBookStage

Day 3:

- ReadCheaply
- ReadingDeals
- GenrePulse

Day 4:

- BookRunes
- EReaderNewsToday
- RobinReads

Day 5:

- RiffleBooks

- KindleBookPromos
- BooksGoSocial
- BooksButterfly

Day 6:

- BuckBooks
- BargainEbookHunter
- BookSends/EReaderIQ

Day 7:

- Your email/FB/LinkedIn again (remind them price goes up and ask for a REVIEW and purchase)
- By now you should be a bestseller in multiple categories - now you increase the price to $2.99 and change the royalty percentage to 70%.

Sample Launch Calendar:

	Monday	Tuesday
Week 1	Email list Facebook/LinkedIn BKnight Bookraid	BargainBooksy BookBongo.com EbookHounds.com eBookStage
Week 2	BuckBooks BargainEbookHunter BookSends/EReaderIQ	Bookzio ManyBooks BookRiot EarlyBirdBooks

	Wednesday	Thursday	Friday
Week 1	ReadCheaply ReadingDeals GenrePulse	BookRunes EReaderNewsToday RobinReads	RiffleBooks KindleBookPromos BooksButterfly
Week 2	Email list Facebook/LinkedIn		

On-Going Marketing:

If you've launched your book properly, you will continue to generate sales after your launch period. But you want to keep on marketing it so it continues to sell well. Below are some of the top methods:

- Amazon ads
- BookBub ads
- Facebook ads
- Pinterest ads
- Get on podcasts in your industry and promote your book(s) on those podcasts
- Local/national media

I'll cover these in section 3 of this book, so keep reading for a deep dive into these because they're necessary to keep selling your book.

What If the Book Flops?

The launch strategy I revealed **works** - but occasionally your book will not perform as expected. In that case, there are a few things to remember:

1. Your book will 99 cents at launch, so royalties will be understandably low - the key is to get consistent daily sales so Amazon can start promoting you
2. You'll be in launch mode, so keep scheduling promotions via the sites that I shared above. Also, share the book with friends, family, etc. Promote on social media, your email list, etc.
3. Use a tool like KindleSpy to see how many sales you need in a day to be a top 20 bestseller in some of your categories. You can easily do 10-20 sales per day at 99 cents and rank even higher.
4. Get as many reviews as you can from friends and family, you should also add the review that I emailed you to your Amazon Author Central account.
5. Consider paid advertising on AMS and possibly even BookBub ads (more expensive though). I'd set a budget of even $5/day.

Positioning and launching the book is the most important part. You have to put a lot of thought into this; if you do, the results will be amazing.

Once you've been a bestseller in your categories for at least one week, you can increase the price to $2.99 and start earning 70% royalties from your Kindle book sales.

Once you understand the process, you can duplicate it and scale it up.

Some of the most successful authors in the world from Stephen King, to EL James, to JK Rowling, to Michael Crichton, to Michael Lewis, to Malcolm Gladwell keep writing more and more books. So you want to do the exact same thing.

I know of self-published authors that earn $15k to $20k per month... their secret is that they keep on writing books.

That's my entire "RWPPPP" process. If you follow it, you'll be able to truly become an elite "authorpreneur", and launch a business from your book.

SECTION 3

The 7 P's of Long-Term Promotion

The Launch *"Hangover"*

If you follow my "RWPPPP" framework, you will most likely have an Amazon bestseller on your hands. It's an exciting achievement and definitely worth celebrating.

You will have lots of exposure, a steady stream of reviews rolling in, and will have people contacting you to inquire about your high-end services.

Take screenshots, share your accomplishments with friends and family, and keep riding the wave because if you do everything correctly, you will enjoy bestseller status for weeks, and even months.

When I launched my first book, *"The Science of Getting Ripped"*, it became a bestseller within a few weeks, and it continued to dominate my categories as a bestseller for months. It was an amazing feeling and something that I was able to replicate over and over again with other books.

My book the *"Passive Income Playbook"* remained a bestseller for months, earning me a pretty penny in royalties and garnering 15-30 new leads for my coaching per day.

Keep in mind that a key strategy of the launch phase is to launch the Kindle version of the book at 99 cents. The key during your launch is to build as much publicity, exposure, and momentum as possible. It will trigger Amazon's algorithm to take notice that the book is selling well, at which point Amazon starts promoting your book for you.

Keep in mind, since the book is only 99 cents, you won't be earning much royalty money (Amazon only offers 35% royalty for books under $2.99), but that's not the objective during this phase. Exposure and momentum is the name of the game during your launch.

After it's a bestseller for at least 10 days, you slowly increase the price to about $2.99, which allows you to earn the full level of royalties from Amazon (70%).

So launching a book is definitely exciting, and you will see incredible results if you follow the "RWPPPP" framework.

But after the launch subsides, your book will inevitably fall off of the bestseller charts. Since the immediacy and excitement of the launch has died down, this is quite natural and to be expected. Also, other new books are released on a daily basis, causing your book to drop down in the rankings.

Authors refer to this as the "launch hangover". It's a time when the euphoria and excitement of the launch has dissipated and you're left with the reality of a book that you've poured your heart and soul into that no one wants to buy anymore.

The key here is to have an active, aggressive, and assertive post-launch marketing plan that uses your book as your means to build authority, a commanding presence, and a dominant voice in your market.

The chapters below are short, but they highlight very simple activities that you can perform to use your book to continue to sell your book, and use that as the way to offer your high-end coaching, consulting, online courses, and speaking.

The 7 P's of Long-Term Promotion:

Now, this brings me to what I call the "7 P's of Long-Term Promotion". Just like the "RWPPPP" framework, I wanted to make it simple and easy for you to understand and remember, which is why I call it the 7 P's of promotion:

- Paid ads
- Partnerships
- Posting on social media
- Press
- Podiums
- Professional associations
- Personal outreach

This is where you take the hard work that you have invested into creating an amazing book, and use it to generate massive exposure, publicity, and credibility for yourself.

The steps that I reveal in the rest of this book work!

You have to have the confidence, boldness, and self-belief to execute. When you do, you'll see some pretty amazing results.

Paid Ads to Promote Your Book *(this is a <u>must</u> for on-going sales)*

Now that your book has launched, you need to keep advertising it to keep it selling. Some of the bestselling books in the world, both traditionally published and self-published, continually sell because of the long-term promotion efforts to constantly keep them in front of readers.

You have to be willing to invest in marketing and promoting your books after the launch so that they keep selling well, and paid ads are a great way to do that.

That said, paid advertising is a skillset of its own, and it requires a tolerance for risk and the willingness to test, tweak, and refine your ads. You'll very rarely earn a profit from your first campaign, so it's important to view each ad and campaign as an experiment.

I actively spend $500 to $1500 per month promoting my books, and it's well worth it; I consistently double my money.

Below is a list of the top paid promotion sites that I use as well as my most actionable advice for each one:

Amazon Ads

- Amazon ads are absolutely _non-negotiable_; the bestselling books in the world use Amazon's advertising system to sell directly to readers

- In my experience, you should expect at least a 50% return on your ads. You can earn even more money if you have high-end services on the backend like speaking, coaching, consulting, and online courses

- Remember to advertise both your Kindle and paperback versions. I know of an author that makes 15k-20k per month from about 30 books; 80% of that revenue is from his paperback books

- I like to manage my own ads, but it's a good idea to hire someone to manage them for you

- Software like PublisherRocket by Dave Chesson is critical because it helps you find amazing keywords with low competition. It also estimates how competitive and profitable those keywords are

- As with any ads, be sure to create multiple ads, use different ad copy, split test, and set a small daily budget that you can eventually scale

- Perfect for full-price books

- Focus on the "Also Bought" section of your book and other similar books

BookBub Ads:

- These are really effective, especially during a launch

- Unlike using Amazon Ads, you will get the best results if you promote deeply discounted books

- The ad creative is KEY; simple and direct works great. You have to spend time creating a really compelling banner ad with stark color contrast and a strong call to action

- You'll get the best results if you target authors and use Cost Per Millieu (CPM) advertising

- BookBub ads are ideal if you publish your book on Apple Books, Barnes & Noble, Kobo, etc.

Pinterest:

- Depending on your topic, Pinterest ads can do really well. Since 80% of Pinterest users are female, it's good to promote books about topics that are of interest to women. The following topics tend to do really well on Pinterest; social media, parenting, food/recipes, blogging, entrepreneurship, fashion, etc.

- Pinterest readers can be impulsive and insanely passionate and often research products on Pinterest before they buy

- Ad clicks are relatively inexpensive; typically less than 20 cents per click

Facebook:

- Facebook ads are incredibly effective and authors are using them to sell their books

- I've seen a lot of people employ a "Free plus shipping" model. They set up a page that offers the book for "free", but the customer covers the $6.95 shipping cost. It works well because they can collect the customer's contact info and use it to send follow-up emails, offering higher end products and services

- I'm not a Facebook ads expert, but if you need help with setting up Facebook ads to sell your books, BookBaby.com has a service that will promote your book on Facebook and Instagram; it's worth checking out

BuySellAds:

- I personally feel like this site a goldmine... it allows you to post banner ads on really popular sites on the internet. Sites like NPR.org, TheAtlantic, and other high-quality websites. They also offer podcast ads and direct email ads

- Just like other ads, they offer CPM ads and allow you to test multiple ad types and formats. The key is to have an eye-catching ad that conveys the value of your book in a way that builds intrigue and curiosity

Quora Ads:

- Quora.com is a popular Q&A site that gets over 300 million users per month. People go to Quora to ask and answer questions, making it an ideal place to promote your non-fiction book

- Some of the world's biggest companies promote their products and services on Quora, so it's definitely worth considering

- I personally have been using it and am constantly testing and tweaking my ad campaigns; I spend anywhere from 18 to 50 cents per click for my ads, but keep in mind that I'm promoting my business website, not necessarily my books. That said, if your book title and cover are compelling enough, you will most likely generate sales, especially if your book is priced at $2.99

- I strongly recommend that you test it out and see if it helps

These are my top tips for promoting your book via paid ads. Of course, there are multiple ad platforms, but these are the ones that I'm most familiar with.

Podcasts Interviews and Partners to Promote Your Book *(this is <u>hot</u>, <u>hot</u>, <u>hot</u>)*

You probably already know that podcasts are **<u>exploding</u>** in popularity these days. I hear about someone launching a new podcast almost every day.

With so many podcasts popping up, there's massive potential to get on and be featured as a guest. Think about it from a podcaster's perspective; they have to constantly create content week after week, so they're always on the lookout for a guest with a great story that they can tell.

Since you'll have a book, you can use that to differentiate yourself from other people that may be contacting them as guests. You can send them a free copy and direct them to your Amazon listing so that they can read your reviews and get a feel for your expertise.

In fact, I've had multiple podcasters purchase my books and contact me to be a guest on their shows; it's that powerful.

One of the other beautiful things about podcasting is that it builds emotional intimacy between the podcaster and the audience. Podcast listeners tend to be very loyal and passionate, and voluntarily spend hours listening to their favorite podcasters; it's really amazing.

The same could be said about other social media platforms like blogs, YouTube channels, Instagram accounts, Facebook Groups, LinkedIn influencers, etc.

The key is to offer something of value to people that already have a massive following and audience. This could be a collaboration like being interviewed on their platform, a joint promotion, writing an article on their blog, or them promoting and sharing your work with their audience.

Your book will differentiate you from the dozens of other people that are contacting them, asking for their attention. If your book is well written, focuses on a specific problem, and tells a great story, you can easily get their attention.

How to Get Featured by Influencers

Getting featured by influencers is relatively simple, it just requires a plan.

Here's the step-by-step process I use:

1. **Make a List**: For my book, "*LinkedIn Sales Machine*", I simply Googled "best sales podcasts" and "top sales podcasts". No matter what your topic is, you can easily do the same thing and compile a list of the top 50-100 podcasts in your industry
2. **Make an Impression**: Now most people try to directly contact the podcasters with cold outreach, but it's not terribly effective. A smarter way is to make an impression on the podcaster by sharing their podcasts on Twitter (tagging them of course) and leave a podcast review. Podcasters live and die by their reviews, so if you leave a thoughtful, intelligent review they'll notice and you'll get their attention.
3. **Make Contact**: AFTER you've made an

impression on them by shouting them out on Twitter, sharing their content, and leaving a review, then you can send them a direct email stating why you love their podcast, how you can help their audience, specific tips that their audience would love, and of course a request to be a guest on their podcast. Here's a sample script I like to use:

"I love your podcast/blog/YouTube videos (as you can probably tell from all of the comments and retweets I've been leaving!)

Anyway, I was wondering how I can help you. You've helped me a lot because _____ and I want to return the favor to you and your audience.

I know they love hearing about _____ and I have a few ideas that could really help them. I even launched a bestselling book about it on Amazon; you can check it out here: [insert link to your book]

Raza

P.S.

I've been working on a really special way to get _____ results. I think it would really help your audience and I'd love to tell you about it.

Simple as that.

One of my clients, Dr. Frazer, really thought out of the box and partnered with an app company to promote his online course; it was a genius strategy.

Now get out there and do the same!

Press and Media *(use your book to become a media celebrity)*

One of my clients was a psychologist that wanted to grow his authority and expertise. He wrote an amazing book called "*The Psychology of Top Talent*" and used it to get on The Morning Joe Show with Joe Scarborough.

He's since gone on to be featured by local media in his area.

Now I'm not a PR expert, but I do know the power of reaching out to local and national media to get attention for your book.

You could hire a PR firm, but if you want to do it yourself, here's a simple plan that you can follow.

1. **Write a Press Release**: I would write a press release and release it on one of the top online press release sites like PRNewsWire or others.

2. **Create a List of Media Outlets that Wrote Articles About Your Industry**: Next, create a list of tv shows, magazines, radio shows, etc. that have written a story about your industry. You can use BuzzFeed.com to identify the top social media posts about these topics as well. Once you do that, you'll have your angle to pitch the media.

3. **Send a Brief, Compelling, Curiosity-Inducing Letter**: Before you do anything, remember that you want to create curiosity. I read about book marketing expert Dave Chilton who sent a letter with two simple sentences on it that got a _tremendous_ response. He didn't send a press release or a free copy of the book, just a letter with two simple sentences that said *"How can a small-town barber help the average person become wealthy?"* Then it said *"For an answer to that question and to setup an interview your listeners will truly love, call..."* He got a 25% response rate to that letter because he built up so much curiosity.

If you're going to reach out to the media, you need to identify stories that they've already run, and then come up with a unique, interesting, intriguing, or innovative angle.

Post on Social Media *(the secret of <u>repurposing</u> your book)*

One of the easiest ways to promote your book is to take snippets and post them on social media.

If you have a book, you already have a wealth of content that you can simply repurpose into bite-sized posts and share them on social media. Of course, you'll want to dig deep into each mini-topic, but if you do it right, you'll have dozens and dozens of content ideas.

Before you get started, here are two of my biggest suggestions:

- **Create a List of Ideas**: Go through each chapter of your book and create a list of ideas. I find the *"Top Problems..."*, *"Coolest Ways to ..."*, *"X Reasons You're Failing at..."* type of pieces do really well. Of course, look at other popular content and model the same headlines and titles. You want to have a list of 10-15 pieces of content that you can create. Doing this simple process will really make your life easy.

- **Batch Your Content**: Now that you have a list of ideas, you want to take some time and batch your content. That means rather than creating one piece of content at a time, you'll create 5-10 at a time and release them later. This is absolutely critical to staying focused and motivated. It's a great feeling knowing that you have a week's worth of content already recorded and written.

Here are great places to repurpose your content, best of all, you can share the same content on multiple platforms.

YouTube Videos:

- YouTube is the second largest search engine on the planet, so you definitely need to take advantage of it
- The key to YouTube is to create really compelling videos, with a "How To" title that solves a real problem

- Be sure to infuse your videos with story, imagery, and emotion so that the viewer is hooked on what you have to say

- Research other popular videos in your industry and pay attention to the titles, descriptions, tags, and comments. Use that info to inform the content that you create

- Include a strong call to action to either buy your book or visit your website

- Be consistent with your videos; commit to publishing a new video once or twice a week

LinkedIn Posts and Videos:

- LinkedIn is really hot these days, which means if your book is about a B2B topic, or relevant to professionals, you need to post your content here

- Creating simple, personal "live" videos that you shoot with your cell phone seem to do really well on LinkedIn

- Gary Vaynerchuck mentioned that engagement on LinkedIn is really strong these days

Pinterest Graphics:

- If Google is the biggest search engine in the world, and YouTube is the second, Pinterest is probably the third; so take advantage of it

- On Pinterest, you can create simple tip graphics or quotes that you can design yourself

- Pay attention to writing strong headlines and having captivating images, because Pinterest is such a visual platform

InstaGram Stories:

- Honestly, I know very little about Instagram, but I know that people are selling their books and programs via InstaGram, so it's worth looking into

Facebook Group Posts:

- Posts in Facebook groups are incredibly effective at building trust and gaining attention

- You want to make a list of the most relevant Facebook groups in your niche and leave helpful comments and insightful posts (don't be promotional)

- Over time, the group will trust you and start contacting you for help. I've made hundreds (and even thousands) of dollars by participating in Facebook groups and I know of people that have made tens of thousands of dollars by being helpful in relevant Facebook groups

- If you make enough of an impression, the group owner may even ask you to do a Facebook Livestream with them

Blog Posts:

- I haven't blogged for years, but now that I have a body of work in the form of books, I could easily take my chapters and subchapters and convert them into blog posts

- Expert marketer Seth Godin said that some of his bestselling books are compilations of blog posts, but you can easily do the opposite and turn your book into separate blog posts

- The key with blogging is to write long posts (2500+ words), tell a story, include bullet points, bold, and italicized text, lots of relevant images, and link to other relevant sites and articles

- Another key is to focus on SEO; that's why you need to pay close attention to your titles and ensure that each title corresponds to a search term that people are actually searching for. There are tons of keyword analysis tools online that help with this, most of them have a free version

- If you have YouTube videos on the same topic, you can also embed them into the blog post

- Of course, don't just copy and paste your book to your blog... modify it and make it unique

Podcast Episodes:

- Just like with videos and blog posts, it's incredibly easy to convert your book into separate podcast episodes (if you have your own podcast)

Twitter:

- Create an optimized Twitter profile with a professional picture and banner image of your book and link to your website or Amazon book page
- Start following other people in your niche, this will cause them to check out your profile. A percentage of those people will click your link and visit your website or buy your book

So that's a brief overview of selling your book by repurposing your content into social media posts. It works really well and will expand your online presence, leading to more sales of your books and more inquiries into your high-end products and services.

Professional Associations and Podiums *(this is how the big dogs do it)*

A friend of mine started a software company for the corporate learning industry and ended up selling it to one of his multi-million dollar competitors. Another guy I knew started a $10 million dollar software company that catered to the insurance industry.

When I asked how they grew their companies, they mentioned that they were involved in industry trade shows, conferences, and professional associations.

In fact, my friend with the corporate learning software company spent upwards of $30k to do joint webinars and email blasts with professional associations.

This is incredibly effective because his ideal market is already associated with these professional organizations and groups, so it just made sense to promote himself there.

I have another friend that started a medical billing software company and he asked for advice on how to market it. Guess what I told him? To identify the top physician associations and trade groups and reach out and look for advertising and sponsorship opportunities.

So let's say you've written a book about human resources or employee engagement. It's a fantastic idea to reach out to the Society of Human Resources Management (SHRM) and look for sponsorships, advertising, speaking, or writing opportunities on their website or at their events.

It doesn't matter what industry you're in, there's likely a professional organization, trade group, conference, convention, or tradeshow that you can participate in.

I'm not saying that you should merely sell your book here, I'm saying that you should use your book to demonstrate your authority and credibility so that you can speak, present, or promote your high-value clients and services.

For example, I have a client that is a Pinterest marketing expert and used a book to be invited to speak at an ecommerce marketing conference. I have another client that used his book to be invited to speak at a social media conference.

The bottom line is that there are multiple venues, teeming with your ideal audience; all you need to do is use your book to prove your authority and expertise so that you can promote your high-value services.

Here are the next steps:

- **Make a List**: The first thing you have to do is make a list of every website, trade group, professional organization, conference, convention, and event in your industry. There are likely dozens of them in your industry.

- **Look for Opportunities**: Spend time on each site looking for advertising, speaking, sponsorship, or writing opportunities. Use your book to demonstrate your expertise on the topic.

It's really that simple. This is how CEO's of software companies that I personally know were able to scale their businesses to multi-millions of dollars in revenue per year.

So find out where your ideal customer is, and participate there!

Personal Outreach *(this is how you <u>really</u> differentiate yourself)*

The other day I was working with a high-end client. She's a healthcare consultant and found me through my book on Amazon. She helps hospitals save millions of dollars in unneeded expenses and is an expert at what she does.

The problem is that she's going up against bigger consulting companies; big firms like Boston Consulting Group, Bain, and McKinsey.

I have another client that's an executive coach. She has an incredible education and corporate background, but she still has to "interview" to be considered by her clients.

I was telling both of them that the best way to differentiate themselves from their competitors is to not only write and launch a book, but to send it directly to their target market.

Here's an example of the process:

1. **Make a List of Your Dream 50 Clients**: Just like in other steps, you need to make a list of the top companies that you want to work with. You can target them by geography, industry, or any other way you want.

2. **Scope Them Out on LinkedIn**: Next, you want to identify the ideal job titles that you sell to; LinkedIn is perfect for this. For example, let's say that you show companies how to sell, you'd simply identify the VP's and Directors of Sales at your target companies.

3. **Send Them Your Book**: Here's where things get interesting. You're going to send a copy of your book, along with a hand-written note explaining that you wanted to work with them. Even more powerful is to send a book to their peers and counterparts. Doing this will definitely build internal buzz and get them talking about you before you even contact them.

4. **Follow-Up**: After you've sent the book, simply send them a LinkedIn invite, send them an email, or call them directly to talk to them and

see how you can help them.

Imagine sending two books out to your ideal clients per week. If your book is well-written and identifies a real problem that they're dealing with, you'll simultaneously gain their attention and edge out your competitors.

Conclusion *(time is of the essence)*

Congratulations, you've made it!

You have everything you need to launch an amazing book that launches your business, but please, please, please, take action.

You've seen the power of writing a book to differentiate you, demonstrate your authority, and attract high-value clients.

You now know my RWPPPP framework for researching, writing, positioning, publishing, promoting, and profiting from a book.

You also know my 7 P's of continuous promotion; paid ads, partnerships, podcasts, posting on social media, press, speaking on podiums, professional associations, and personal outreach.

If you follow my system, you can have a bestselling book written and launched with less than 24 hours of "work".

I knew these steps for years, but I procrastinated and didn't take aggressive, persistent action. Instead, I was lulled into complacency and inaction.

Don't be like me.

You're an expert with high-value skills. Now turn that expertise into a book that launches a highly-profitable business that allows you to make an impact.

So now it's up to you to take action.

Imagine telling your friends and family that you wrote a bestselling book.

Imagine getting invited to speak at events, be interviewed on podcasts, and to write for large publications based on your book.

Imagine selling courses, and coaching, and consulting packages.

Imagine quitting your job and living life on your own terms.

That's all possible for you if you take **ACTION**.

So, put what you've learned to work and make it happen.

Recommended Resources

Here are my absolute favorite resources. I personally use them and can't recommend them enough.

I make a commission if you buy any of these products, but I would recommend them even if I didn't - plus, you're getting a massive discount on these tools.

They'll make your life easier and help you get your business started in a matter of days.

1. **Domain Names and Web Hosting: HostGator**
   They have incredible customer service and make setting up a blog a breeze.
   Click here for my special discount bundle offer for $3/month:
   http://www.authorpreneurelite.com/hostgator
2. **Wordpress Theme: ThriveThemes**
   Some of the world's most popular non-fiction

authors also have a blog. An excellent way to get more book sales and consulting clients is to repurpose parts of your book as blog posts. I highly recommend Thrive Themes because they have very sophisticated, business-friendly themes.

You can watch their video here:

http://www.authorpreneurelite.com/thrivethemes

3. **Amazon Market Research Tool: KindleSpy**

I can't recommend this tool enough. In a matter of seconds, it tells you how profitable and how competitive a category is. This makes market research incredibly easy.

If you buy a tool, this should be the one; it's a complete game-changer:

http://www.authorpreneurelite.com/kindlespy

Need Advice? Reach Out To Me

If you need personal advice on your project, feel free to contact me in one of the following ways:

Email: Feel free to email me at

raza.imam@authorpreneurelite.com

Facebook Group: Feel free to join my free Facebook Group

http://authorpreneurelite.com/fbgroup

LinkedIn: Feel free to connect with me and ask me questions on LinkedIn at

www.LinkedIn.com/in/razasimam

Book a Call: If you want to schedule time for me to give you personal advice (*for free*), feel free to book time on my calendar here

www.authorpreneurelite.com/discovery-call

How I Can Help

In "*AuthorPreneur Elite*", I show you *exactly* how to launch a book that allows you to sell high-value services - FAST. If you follow these steps, you'll see incredible results.

But it takes a **solid plan**, **consistent work**, and **persistence**.

If you need help with the ***inevitable*** pitfalls, obstacles, and roadblocks you'll face, then I offer two things coaching to help:

- **AuthorPreneur Elite Course**: This is a 7-module course that walks you through exactly how to do this

- **AuthorPreneur Elite Coaching**: This is my group coaching program where I work with you to identify your topic, position it, write it quickly, launch it, and profit on the backend.

You also get a copy of the course if you purchase my coaching.

I'll personally help you launch your book so you can earn royalties from your book and grow your income with consulting, coaching, and speaking.

Just email me at raza.imam@authorpreneurelite.com or watch the video here:

www.AuthorPreneurElite.com

Before You Leave a Review…

Thank you again for buying and reading this book. If you got this far, it's because you finished the book, so congratulations!

Authors live and die by the reviews we receive from our readers. So if you liked this book, I'd really appreciate if you left it a 5-star review.

If you didn't like this book, <u>before you leave a negative review</u>, please email me at <u>raza.imam@authorpreneurelite.com</u> and let me know what you would like me to improve. The beauty of publishing online is that I can instantly add content, fix errors, and update information.

So if there's something you didn't like, or that you'd like me to remove, please email me so I can fix it.

Thanks!

Made in the USA
Las Vegas, NV
30 December 2021